THE *Spiral Staircase* OF *My Life*

A Selection of Poetry Defining My Thirty Years

Dominick Rizzo

authorHOUSE®

AuthorHouse™
1663 Liberty Drive, Suite 200
Bloomington, IN 47403
www.authorhouse.com
Phone: 1-800-839-8640

First published by AuthorHouse 12/22/2008

ISBN: 978-1-4389-2102-0 (sc)
ISBN: 978-1-4389-2103-7 (hc)

Printed in the United States of America
Bloomington, Indiana

This book is printed on acid-free paper.

Contents

To my Lovely Wife,
Thank You for being so strong when I was so weak

To my Sons,
Thank You for teaching me to slow down and enjoy life

To my Family,
Thank You for picking me up off the mat,
when I was almost down for the count

A Special Thank You to
David Duncanberger and The Iron Shop
for the front cover photograph

Only remember

Only remember that I love you
Nothing is as special as our love
Only wish you would remember
No matter what I do, what I become
How far apart we find ourselves
I will always love you
I wish you would remember me
Loving you

Only promise me

Promise me you will count the stars
With me tonight
I cannot be with you
Please share this secret moment
With me tonight
Stand on your porch
I will walk down your street
Maybe we will gaze upon the same star
With your image reflecting off of the brightest
If the sky holds no stars
I will know without understanding
Why I am all alone tonight

If I were

If I were to buy you flowers for a lifetime
Would you love them?
If I were to buy you jewels every week
Would you cherish them?
If I were to buy you the world to keep forever
Would you call it your own?
If I were to buy you a wedding ring tomorrow
Would you keep it in your heart?
If I were to hold you in my arms tonight
Would you truly love me?

Ordinary words

We always say goodbye
But hope to see each other again someday
Years go by, faces come and go
Hello, goodbye
Just ordinary words
Until a blind and deaf man
Comes and steals them away.

No longer

Here I stand
Away from land
So high, I cannot feel
The blood rushing through me like a flood
I take off for flight
Searching for that certain light
Instead I am struck with cold dark waters
My pain is gone, I am no longer

Simple inquiry

What is this place that my eyes have just seen?
Where might I be?
So I may find you
And bring you there with me
This place of peace and love
I have found
Where might you be?
My love, I have searched and cannot find
Where might you be so you may come with me and see

Open bottle of red wine

On the counter from the night before
Such love and passion spoiled
Broken vase and flowers on the floor
Open bottle of red wine
Two empty glasses with no taste of
Rose petals on the bed
Wilted from hours of neglect
No one around, no one else here
On the counter from the night before
Such love and betrayal shared
Written letter from her to him
Laying under the bottle of red wine
A loss of love from one to the other
Rose petals have long since died
Put to rest by hands and a black bag
No one around here, no one else here

What I want to be

What I want to be
Is everything you want to find out there
If you need love, let me be love
If you are after romance, so let me be
If you need kindness, let me be the kind you need

I only want to be with
Everything I am is for you
Only you
What I want to be
Is everything you cannot find out there

Look through the window

Maybe you will see forever
Or could it only be tomorrow?
Look through the window
Maybe you will find your treasure waiting for you
If you find the rainbow, you are almost there

Maybe you will see the face you have
    searched all the yesterdays for
Or could it only be a shadow?
Look through the window
Maybe you will see what could have been

Maybe all you see is everything and nothing
All at the same time
Look through the window
Can it be yesterday fading and tomorrow elevating
While today stands still
Look through the window
The rainbow you have searched for
Has just fallen

Someday, not today

Someday, not today
I will find true love
And what it truly means to be happy
Someday, not today
I will forget who I was
And realize who you really were
Someday, not today
I will know what to say
And not have to hide from the
    truths of yesterday
Someday, not today
My true love will say goodbye and
    suddenly leave me, again
And I will turn around and fly away
Someday, not today

Green arm

This addiction I cannot break
Like a mad man in his chains
There really is no escape from this
Maybe someday I will ask for help
But now, it is not worth my life to stop
The high, the rush, the pleasure
With each needle push
Dreams are reality
And I cannot live my life without

This addiction has broken me
Like a war torn soldier
There was escape I just could not see
Now I ask for help
But now my life is worth even less
The high, the rush, the arm
With each needle push
Reality is all too clear
And I cannot believe my life without

My only fear

The darkness is my only
Not the blackness of the night
Or even the lost feeling of being me
But the emptiness of never again to have
My only fear is searching without ever finding her light

The darkness is my only
Not the coldness of my bedroom walls
Or even the sad image of me
But the extinguished light I am sure to find
My only fear is discovering her abandoned light

Déjà vu

The time has come to sleep and dream of tomorrow
Watch the pictures unfold before you in your mind
If you can keep your eyes closed long enough
You just might wander further into a land of make believe

The time has come to awake and wander through the day
Things you see for the first time
You know you have seen before
Welcome to your life's reality
You never forget your dreams and you never want to leave

The time has come once again to say goodnight
Watch the lights go out from window to window
Candles are blown out in praise of the night
For you never know what you may see
Welcome to your mind's reality
Where what you see in your dreams
creates your make believe

All for you

What is it you wish to find here?
Roads of marble with no cracks
Houses of stone, with no sign of brick
Just what do you need to see here?
Sunny days with no rain
Clear skies with no sign of clouds

All this is for you
Written out just for you
Take my wrinkled hand
I will show you your new home
It is just around the corner

Who is it you wish to be here?
Mr. invisible with only false friends
Mr. know it all with all your books
Just what do hope to hide from here?
Ugly skeletons living and dying in your closets
The past of your most recent life you
        hope to forget all about

All this is for you
Scripted out just as you requested
Take my boney hand
I will show you your new home
It is just around the corner

The joker

Have you ever wondered why the
    joker is always smiling?
Is it the pure shape of his lips?
Or does he know something you do not?
Maybe he just made love with your wife
And now he laughs in your face
As you shake your head "no" in denial

Have you ever wondered why the
    joker always paints his face?
Is it because he hates himself?
Or does he hide behind his colors?
Maybe he has been your lover for a month
And a killer for three
Now he paints his face a different shade of red
As you slowly fall asleep

Jack or Jill

I think I need some more
Either you or the bottle
Does not matter much to me
I am in love with the both of you
My heart beats faster, and my blood feels hot
All I know is you are over there
And I am out of Jack

I know I need some more
Maybe you more than the bottle
Maybe the bottle more than you
I am addicted to the both of you
My lips anticipate as my world just spins
All I really know is you are over there
And I am out of Jack

Rain, rain stay another day

I met her in the rain
She was just standing there
With her beautiful face tilted to the sky
Said her name was love
And she loved being in the rain
When I asked her why
She smiled, then she laughed
She danced naked in the street
We made love until the rain stopped
Then she began to cry
The sun chased her rain away
She just turned and ran away
I cursed the sun
Then caught loves last raindrop

Remember when

Take my hand
We can walk together
Yesterday's path is by the river
I know it has been a long time since
Let us go now before it gets too dark
Remember when we would watch
    the water roll onto the sand
I was lost in your eyes, you could only laugh
Remember each kiss, each kiss just like the first
Remember just being together, only us

Let me wipe your tears away,
I am to blame for your sadness
Yesterday's eyes have now replaced my own
Come on let us keep walking up this hill
Remember when you said, " I love you"
Remember when I would touch your
    face only to believe you were real
Remember my love, remember when

Old man is me

Sat down next to me
Shook my hand
Said he knew me
"The war, my son, it was rough"
He let go of my hand
Then he began to cry
He waved his hand in the air
"When I returned home, my wife of
    ten years had said goodbye"
He said he never again had
Then I watched him walk away
He said he knew me
Some time went by
I sat and wondered
Then I began to cry

Wiseman and me

Wiseman stared at me
I knew he did not like me,
My darkness shadows his world
And may I add, his sunlight shines too bright

We talked for a while
He would never admit to it
But he was like me
And I like him
Sometimes the sun hides behind dark clouds
Sometimes the moon shines brightly through the night

When she walked away

When she walked away
I knew I would never see her again
Lost like a dream
I could barely remember
Who I was before we fell in love

When she walked away
She turned back only to wave goodbye
Lost like a kiss
I could feel myself begin to break

When she walked away
I felt a soft touch on my shoulder
Lost like a fallen leaf
I could not realize who had just touched me
The one I would love forever had just said, "Hello"

Wooden tables

If you want to find me
I will be in the woods
Burying the hatchet
And digging up my grave
Just listen for the rustling of the leaves
And the noisy shovel in the dirt

If you need to find me
I will be in the woods
Burying the shovel
And covering my body
Just listen for the wind blowing through the trees
And the noisy demons taking me away

Do you need to hear such words?

Do you need to hear
Those words of love everyday and night?
Can your love breathe without hearing such
Or does a part of it die
When he only nods his head and smiles
Why do you need to hear such words?
Do they really mean more to you
Than when he buys you purple roses
Or are the words all you need
To rest your head and sleep at night?
If I never said those gentle words
Would you love me because
Such words are so distant to me
And I may never say such words again
But the purple roses are laying on the bed

Surprise visit

You will not find her here
And you will not find her there
Do not challenge destiny
Or what your book has been scripted
Never forget who you really are
And she will never know who you could have been

You may find her here
And you may find her over there
Live the life you are to live
Walk the path you are to see
Always remember you are never alone
All it takes is one glance, one moment, one surprise visit

Have never seen

I have never seen beauty
I have been told what it looks like
And even where I may find
But even if I did go wander off in search of
What would I look for?
I do not know where beauty hides
Do you? Do you really know?
Could you take me there and show me
Because I have looked here and cannot find
Maybe my eyes do not go as deep as yours
Maybe your eyes see more than mine
Because I cannot find where beauty lies.

The Drunken Satyr

When the fawn dances
There is only music
No other sound can be heard
The Drunken Satyr drinks 'til he is sober
Then he drinks some more
This monster of a man has forgotten his ugliness
Does not see beauty sparkle in the female eye
This now sober but soon drunk man
    wanders through the forest
In search of her and her love
He has personified the lust for life
Only to recognize love in it's purest form
So he may be drunk in love

Bridge of memories

I just found myself
Sitting here all alone
Do not know where I was
Or if I was even lost
Maybe I never left this place
But if I did go, then where were my eyes
Maybe I was all the way over there
Someplace, anyplace, a place lost in time
Where if I did go
And if I did have eyes
I would find myself again
Sitting there with you

This is what it is

Nothing more
Nothing less
Given all I have
Taken only what I can carry
Forgotten all that I have lost
Have said goodbye without ever
    looking into their eyes
I do not know if I will ever see them again
This is what it is

Nevermore
Never less
You can have all I have
If you can take what I decide to give
Forget what you have lost
Resurrect the cemetery's past
And all the skeletons that live there
This is what it is

Light post

The light post shines
A bright light on the rain soaked road
She and I walk together
Holding hands only to stop
And kiss under
The moonlight that shines her love
Opposite the light post

She pulls away suddenly
I hate when she pulls away from me
She and I so different
Even holding hands
I can feel her love hide from me
The moonlight that shines opposite the light post
Has begun to burn out

Look and see

Look and see
And you may find me here alone
Always outside
Never inside
Knocking on the window
Trying to be seen

Look and see
And quickly turn away from me
Always ignore the truths
Never deny the lies
My constant knocking has just shattered the window
You should have never looked into these eyes

Come with me

Come with me
I can show you where tomorrow hides
Alone in a cave
He creeps along the cliff's edge
Waiting for the moon to go away
Only the sun can welcome him in
With a nod and an unrehearsed blink
The new day upon us

Come with me
I can show you where yesterday hides
Alone in a cave, on the other side
He cries along the cliff's edge
Remembering his old friends
Now his tears fall from his eyes in a constant stream
Look over there, below the cliff's edge
See there, the beautiful waterfalls

Purple Roses

Have you seen them?
My wife only likes the purple roses
Not the red or the yellow
But only the purple
She says they smell different
I do not know
I just like to see her smile

I saw them first
Bought them for her wrapped in white paper
Not for the dancer or the mother I once had
But for her
She says they remind her of violets, but with thorns
I cannot tell
I just like to see her smile

Sleepwalker

Turtle on the train tracks
Can he hear the whistle blowing?
Soon to be heard forever
Have you forgotten where you placed your happiness?
Does music still orchestrate in your mind?
Angry waters crashing into rocks
Swordfish left flapping on the dock
Blackness cannot be seen
Can you remember where your dreams took you?
Mirror hanging on the floor
Do not touch the art pieces
No flash photography, white is all you can see
Will it be this time or the next time
Bumblebee stuck to sticky bug tape
Sad raindrops fall from the sky, metal poles prohibited
Can you tell me where are all the flowers
Released serial killer kills again, who do
    you want to be for Halloween?
And where does your tomorrow lead you,
    somewhere near the train tracks?

Next to her

In love with her
I am a better man
Only to be a stronger man
Next to her
There are always sunny days with rainy days
Next to her
My only fear is losing her
I swear I can hear the angels sing her name
Next to her
I only wish her to be happy
In love with her
I only see her laughing at me
Next to her
I am completely in love with her

Surgery

Metal on metal
Waves of life
Red on white
Water of life
Bright light on closed eyes
Clock of time
Maybe ticking away

Steady hand on hand
Thunder of death
Red on white, then more red
Lightning of death
Darkened cape closes open eyes
Clock of time
Has just expired

Only anyone to be

Only anyone to be someone
Never to truly understand yourself
Always searching for the truth
When all you recognize are lies
To look in the mirror
And wonder who is hiding behind
Only yourself to be someone else

Only someone to be anyone
Never to be completely happy with you
Always trying to change the truth
When all you are doing is creating the lies
To shatter the mirror
And realize you were hiding behind
Only anyone to be nothing else

Pictures on the wall

Just hanging there
Staring into nothing
Man who hung them long since dead
Pictures on the wall
Whisper a thousand words
As if they speak through him
I can just barely hear his last words

Just hanging there
Staring into darkness
Man who hung long since dead
Nightmares on the wall
Flash a thousand photographs
As if they watched him with his own eyes
I can just barely see his twisted face

Down the tunnel

I have been here forever
Warning all men who enter
Down the dark, narrow tunnel
Of a woman dressed in black
Who awaits in the shadows
If you can avoid her glance, she may decide to spare you
Her eyes that can see forever and never die
Will forever blind you
A breath of her stale air will whisper evil into your ears
never mind the red shadows on the brick walls
Dried purple stains from so long ago
The muddy ground, how even it cannot escape
Is trampled beneath her barefeet
While the man finds imprisonment inside her
Dim lights from ancient lanterns flash a bright light
every time she feels his tension and pulsating
Her screams are deafened only by his
I told them like I tell you
But they saw beauty and could not deny
Now these men have breathed their last
And now cannot be found
If you can escape her, by not seeing her
The silver bridge
will take you to the most beautiful waterfalls known to man

Who was I?

Maybe there have been days
When I was not me
When I lied to myself
And tried to be someone else
Hidden me in the closet
While I wore another face
A brand new smile had worn out
Only a fake smile and silent eyes
Felt as close to real as I could ever have

Maybe there have been months
When I was a stranger
When I deceived even my mother
And forgot who I once was
Hidden my mind in a tunnel
While my legs walked around this world
An old emotion could never die
Only a real sense of loss and a battle to continue
Has now created a new

Maybe now there is a future
When I can finally be me
When I can finally be true
And let them and you inside
Hidden my dark eyes in a coffin
While my new eyes have just been born
A brand new vision to be seen
Only a real smile has brought me back here
So I may finally see myself again

The ocean is a woman

The ocean is a woman
Her beautiful waves in and out of her tides
Dancing night and day
Low tide, high tide
The moonlight that shines on her
Create her emotions
Sometimes getting the best of her
Her cool salty foam of perfume on top
She blankets the earth for as far as the eye can see
Such comfort to the mountains
With her soft loving caress of her hips against the rock
Sometimes only to tease
But usually so they know she is still there
The ocean is a woman
Because the sky is a man

The sky is a man

The sky is a man
Can you imagine it any other way?
His blue skin so bright
Dotted with so many clouds
His brother, friends around him
He stands so proud, aware of all he has
So quick to turn, his emotions upside down
With no warning of
Dark skies shout out his lightning
His fist pounds out the thunder
Tears of guilt and sadness fall from above
The cool blue ocean accepting, even inviting her forgiveness
Forgetting what he has done
The sky is me
Because the ocean is my wife

No reason to wait

Does the corruption I see
Create my isolation?
In turn develop only a tolerance to it all
My constant meditation has been
    a source of relaxation
But my constant hallucinations have
    been a cause for medication
So I ask where does depression
    sit among all of this?
Can it be constant gratification to
    assume these sensations?
An extreme justification to the
    assassination of the population

Does the clarification I impose upon
Destroy accusations?
In response eliminate the execution
    and destruction of the world?
Is it only I that can see a solution?
All by the filtrations of fornications
    through our glorifications
Or are we destined to live forever in
    this world of hallucinations
Through a time of freezing crystallization
where nothing can be seen, felt or embraced

Dirt of my honor

Color of my mind
Dirt of my honor
Covered in mud
From top to bottom
Not that I care
Cannot say that I do
I will create the lies
You try to break down
Continue to develop the false ideas
You try to tear away

Color of my blood
Dirt of my honor
Covered in shame
From him to me
Not that I know him
Will not say that I do
He will create the truths
I try to destroy
He will share new memories
I try to ignore

Snake bit

She asked who wrote the song
That made her cry
When I told her it was I
She cried some more
Such a sweet girl, I made cry
And she wanted to know why
How could I write such a sad piece
And why did I have to make her cry
When I told her it was written for her
She smiled with beautiful eyes
Such a sweet girl, I made smile
And now she knew why
Why I wrote the song that made her cry

Bother no one

Moonlight shines
Sunlight burns
Emotions are too strong
Blood tastes bitter
Sugar tastes sweet
Loneliness stems from being alone
Roses stem from light green thorns
These flowers grow alone
I do not think they like all the others
Their thorns divide

Bedroom light shines
Closet light burns
Nightmares are never wrong
Blood tastes salty
Sugar taste is always sweet
Madness stems from being all alone
Roses stem from long green thorns
The flowers never care who hold them
I do not think they like to be held
Their thorns divide

The coffin is waiting

The coffin just sits in the corner
Open doors only to be closed
Soft pillow patiently awaits for the indentation forever
Loved ones have all been notified
Soon to be filled both coffin and new hole
With the empty cavity of a man
Closed eyes, still heart and frozen body
The coffin just sits in the corner

The coffin, now moved, sits in a small room
Open doors cannot wait to be closed
Soft pillow accepts the stillness of the mind
The loved ones gathered all around
Soon to be covered both coffin and new hole
With what was once a breath of man
Open gates, still images and frozen soul
The coffin just sits in a small room
The coffin is waiting

The sun that would not shine

Climbed the highest mountain
Almost like I was climbing a brick building
Asked the sun to come out from hiding
Shook his head no and hid behind the clouds
Asked him why
Like a child he began to cry
I tried to dry his soaked eyes
Burned my hands instead
Said he was sorry, but he could not
    escape the fire around him

Climbed down, what felt like the smallest mountain
Almost as if I was climbing out of a tree
Wondered why the sun could not
    come out from behind
Shook my head in sadness, then smiled
    and began climbing the rock
Told him why
Like a child in the morning he
    opened his dreamy eyes
I dried his soaked eyes
Ignoring the burning feeling on my hands
Said he was sorry, again, for the burns,
I only laughed and admired the fire around him

Plastic clay

Leave me alone
My walls painted red
Plastic clay on my mirror
Cannot see reflections
No more sadness
Maybe time to leave
Hour of death awaits
Hand of nakedness feels so much
Glove of covering hides so much
Cannot feel touch
Smell of paint and food
Plastic clay on my plate
No more death wish
Maybe too late now
Poor man begging for some change
Plastic clay molded to his hands
No more shadows in my closet
His gloves of covering are hidden there
Cannot see his true identity staring
    through my mirror
Left alone with desires
Forgotten faces never seen again
Wish it was not time to leave
Plastic clay

May I

When I cared so much
Everything was shameful
When I watched so carefully
Everything fell from the shelf
When I loved and was devoted to
I lost everything I held so close to me
So now I ask
May I care for you
So I can start all over
May I be with you
So I can begin to put the pieces back
May I love you
So I can remember what I once had

When I tried so hard
The pieces never fit together
When I gave so much passion to
The object of my desire burned in the flames
When I wanted to save my love
She only walked away
So now I ask again
May I ask you to join me
To pick up the broken glass that has fallen beside
May I ask you to stand by me
While I put away the fires
May I ask you to remember me
Because I may be leaving here real soon

Anna

Funny how some girls can make you feel
Only to leave you so soon
With that lost feeling
Desires left dangling from the sky
Love we could have felt and learned to recognize
Is always there, we just ignore it all
Sometimes it only takes a glance
Most of the time that is all we really need
All the other times are wasted wondering

Funny how our lives come together
She lived way over there, away from me
I lived all the way over here, away from her
Met her no where near here or there
Will probably never see her again
Even though she left me with the desire
Hers and mine
To feel completely in love
Funny how some girls can make you feel

What I like to see burn

By my hands
The memory of all
To finally let go
Never to return
Destroyed thoughts linger in the smoke
Disappear in clouds
of what I like to see burn
By my breath
Your words are never heard
And released instead the guilt and
    denial through the pleasures
Of what I like to see burn

Hidden treasures

It is what it is
To feel so fake inside
All reasons why
To be taken
Something so special taken away

It is only
It is what it is not
No reason to think otherwise
Because it was so important to me
To let go is to forget the past
But what if the past will not go?
Where do you go when you cannot stay?
Can you forgive the unforgivable
Only to accept the past for what it was?
And what the future can be?
To go on without, to be taken
Only to have to forget, so you can move on
And forgive those who have taken so much

Tiger lily

It's what tomorrow is
And what yesterday was not
Wondering what will become
And maybe I think too much
Maybe I wonder too much
But yesterday is gone
Like lonely goodbyes that sadly had to be spoken
But tomorrow has yet to come
Like a wave that has yet to crash into the sands of time
And maybe I think too much
Maybe I love too much
But yesterday was
And tomorrow can be so much more

Amber

Her name was like the beautiful sky
Her face so innocent
Reminded me of love
She was full of beauty and full of life
I talked to her once, only once
Like the rain, she came and went
I wish she would return

Her name was Amber
Such beautiful colors lit up my world
She so beautiful
Like a rainbow after the rain
I saw her again,
She had to go and could not talk
I said nothing
Like a burned out star I closed my eyes
I wish she would return

Red 55

The color of evil
Has blackened the earth
The red cape that cascades below
Has burned out the stars
Guilty eyes closing one last time
Evil in complete horror
Of the red cape that disguises
The unveiling of the truth of evil and guilt

Don't read this

Don't read this
My empty mind has opened
Dangerous thoughts into this my book of wonder
If you read this
My empty mind will be no longer
I will destroy such book silently
My Skeleton on the chair will tear the pages into shreds
While trees sway from side to side like each page turning
Gates open and close, making a cracking
    sound like a rocking chair
I told you not to read this
My terrified eyes have been closed
Dangerous vision into this my book of wonder
You read this,
My terrified eyes will be no longer
I have destroyed such book blindly
My skeleton sitting on the porch
A swing sways back and forth like a weeping willow
Wooden doors open and close like a mouth screaming from
    an empty room where I, a skeleton sit in a rocking chair
Reading this, my book of wonder

Heroine

Lost forever in a world of emptiness
I see the colors of the rainbow
And then darkness overwhelms me
My hair is long and dirty
My throat burns from this liquor
I sit up against the wall because I am tired of sleeping
And my legs cannot support me, I cannot support myself
My arms bleed, they burn like a thousand bees stinging me
I insert my relief, my eyes are closing
Maybe for an hour or two
Maybe forever
I am too lost to care
My memory has faded, I have forgotten who I am
Lost in a world of emptiness

The song plays on:

The song plays on, memories of riding on
Only to bring me back here, where I always was
Had to leave here to release anger
Only to find love and then anger again
These emotions just flow and flow
I do not know where they come from or what they mean
This has stained me and this has hurt me
The song plays on and on with the memories fading
All I see is this, all I know is anger and love
If I ever leave this place of horror,
I will come see you and the ocean you hide behind
Where dreams are made and these places die,
I feel this way forever, I cannot breathe
And I cannot understand them and all the others
What they mean and who they really are
All this has stained me, all this has hurt me
The song plays on and on, memories riding on
With always the same words, but different meanings
I do not understand much of anything anymore

Dedicated to Dominick Figliomeni

No emotions

She asked me why I never say I love you
And why I never smile
She asked me who I really was
And why I never cared where I was going
She asked me if I had ever cried
And if I knew what it was to be in love

She asked me why I never laugh
And why I never remember her words
She asked me who will you become
And why don't you care who you really are
She asked me if I had ever cried
Or if I really knew what it was to be in love

My box of confidence

I keep thinking she will come back to me
Creep up behind me
whisper my name with hers
To tell me she is back, that she missed me
I keep seeing her face
And cannot stop thinking of her
Her face, her hair, her love
Falling in love with me once again
I keep thinking she will

When tomorrow comes

When tomorrow comes
Maybe I will not be here
Lost somewhere else, not lost here
But losing my mind between worlds
When day breaks

When the new day shines, hopefully I will not
Dulled by the new sun light
Forgotten between crowds, never again here
but losing everything I ever had
And never knowing what I could have
Maybe I will be dead
When tomorrow comes

Beauty

What is beauty?
Can ugly be beauty?
If I was jaded would I be?
As you see me now, am I?
How far does beauty go?
Is it above the cover or below the cover?
Is black beauty, is sadness beauty?
And if it is beautiful, when does it stop being?
Only to become something else
Are words beauty?
They paint scenes in our minds
Can I erase them even if they are?
Do they ever die or do they continue to live?
Does beauty make you sad?
Can these words be beautiful
        even if the writer is not?

Two dead birds

The truth frightens the guilty
The guilt that lives in me frightens the truth
Every shivering moment
Every deafening hour
I fear what it beholds
Two dead birds in a cage
A masked man frightens the lady
The truth frightens the innocent
The innocence that once lived in me has died
With every lost emotion
With every deadened tear
I see all too clear what it beholds
Two dead birds flapping their wings in a cage
An unmasked man, a son, frightens his mother
The truth, the truth frightens us all

Somewhere

Love lost somewhere
Kissed goodbye and then gone
Forgotten then remembered
But only for a moment
Ashamed maybe
Hurt always
Love lost somewhere

Love lost somewhere else
Blown away from the palm of his hand
Remembered then forgotten
But only for a moment
Devastated definitely
Hurt always
Love lost somewhere else

The quiet one

He is gone now too
The quiet one has walked away
Joined his long departed friend
The one who imagined too much
Joined now by the quiet one
A man of beautiful lyrics of Something
And guitars that weep so gently

He is gone far far from here
The quiet one has nothing left to say
Joined his long haired friend
The one who loved too much
Joined now by the quiet one
A creator of beautiful words of promises
And scenes of children pointing to the sun

Fantasies of her love

The moonlight shines throughout the night
A seductive thunder is heard
Rain cascading upon
The broken bridge creeks eerily
While we pass above
Following shadows throughout the lost and remembered
Fantasies of her love
Her soft hands and coffee breath
Has brought me back to reality
Deep inside I know this is all
This is all I will ever really have

Never fear

Never fear
The darkness that surrounds you
Never fear
The shadows that lurk around you
Never fear
The deafened silence that makes you shiver
Never fear
The breath that happens to breeze by you
Never fear
The constant voice that engulfs you
Never fear
Her soft touch on your naked body

She is the darkness you cannot ignore
She is the shadow you want to hide from
She is the silence you wish so much to break
She is the breath you want only to inhale
She is the voice you will never forget
She is the touch on your naked body that terrifies you

All in my hands

Everything and then nothing at all
All in my hands
All through my hands
Always thought I could hold on to
Never thought I would drop it all
Always thought it would cradle in my hands

Nothing and then everything will fall
From my hands
All through my hands
Always thought I could catch it all
Never thought I would drop it all
Always thought I could cradle it in my hands

But beyond all that

When I am alone
My thoughts escape me
When I am alone
My thoughts consume me
Each time filling me with grief
Beyond understanding
So over flown with self doubt
I have sharpened the razor's edge against my chin
Only the lame blade has saved my life
Leaving behind tiny scratches that bleed and bleed
Ever slowly, droplets of blood
Reminding me, I am no use anymore
My own blood cannot wait to escape me

Shelter

I do not think you would understand
Such words of lost emotions
Given away to such lies and deception
Nothing is as real as it seems
It is an illusion to think otherwise
This life is a game of winners and losers
Mostly losers and I am king of them all
The losers follow me as if I know something
Funny as it is, all I truly know, I just do not know

I do not think you want to believe
Such thoughts of desperation
It is impossible for you to journey on with me
My caravan of losers has become full, too full
Full of emptiness I must now carry
Carry on my broken back, a painful
    reminder of the delusion of me
That ultimately has become my life
I think now you finally understand
Now you finally believe
Only now it is too late

Moving on

I am drunk with fear
And I am drowning in a sea of tears
Pushed you away over and over again
They say I will be alright
They say this is all going to be okay
I am not so sure
I am not so happy anymore

I am stoned and numb from fear
And I am swallowing life by the dozen
Pushed myself to the edge again and again
You say it will be alright
You say this is all going to pass
I am not so sure I will not jump this time
I am not so happy anymore

What he told me

The 85 year old Wise Man once told me
The Good Lord has blessed Me
With a Beautiful Wife and a Beautiful Life
I have lived to see my Great Grandchild
And the growth of my Grandchildren

He smiled deeply and proudly
When it is time to go
I only hope you will all understand
It is His will
A Selfless Man sat among his faith
Atop a small desk with His Prayer
    Cards, Saint Cards
And a Bible, a Bible so close to Him
    it was beating in His Heart
His love overflowing
His need to help others unending
The Wise Man was perfect
A Servant of God,
He now sits among the Angels in Heaven
Watching over us all

Dedicated to my Grandfather

Message from Heaven

Wherever you are
I think of you
whenever I forget to remember
You think of me
The phone call with no one on the other end
A sudden fallen picture of, falling from the wall
The gentle wind on the face, no one else feels
And sometimes the third time, really is the charm
Wherever you have gone
I wish to be someday
Whenever I remember too much
You think of me
That tiny voice that came from somewhere
A sudden rainstorm followed by a rainbow
The gentle touch on the shoulder
    thought to be our imagination
And sometimes the third time, really is the charm

Arrogance, hers and mine

Pardon me
I was lost in a thought
Or was it a dream?
Who can really tell?
And who wants to really know?
I saw her there just before her face melted away
Leaving droplets on the floor and
  her hand print on my door
She ran away blindly
I watched through the window
Her face in her hands, my laughter
  so loud, it made her cry

Excuse me
I was lost in space
Or was it time?
What is the difference?
And what does it really matter?
I saw her years later just before she passed away
Leaving thoughts on my mind and
    her memories in my eyes
She had gone away forever
I watched through the window
My head in my hands, her laughter
    so loud, it made me cry

Smashed bottle

I am sorry dad
You saw me drinking
Smashed bottle
I do not know what I was thinking

My thinking is my drinking
And my drinking is my way of life

Happiness in this world
Troubles in my life
Hidden beneath the shattered ruins
of a broken bottled life

My pile of emotion

Can you tell me who have I become
Because I do not think I know anymore
My own face, my own image
I cannot recognize
Can you help me see them
Because I think I have lost my eyes
Never to see again
Will you help them see me
Because I feel so invisible
As if I was born into this life
Never to be seen
Can you help them see me
Because I feel so empty inside
Can you tell me who I really am

Has it been

Has it been a dream?
A dream I cannot remember
This unfortunate life
Somehow Intwined like a spider's web
Before I close the door to my bedroom
Who have I let in?
And who will never leave?

Has it all been a nightmare?
A nightmare I just cannot wake up from
This sad life
Somehow built to break me
After I shut the light in my bedroom
Who stares at me from across my bed
And who nods their head as I fall asleep?

13 years ago

Where am I in the shadows?
My white curtain has fallen from above
Maybe the final end
Just the beginning to something new
Another place to see
In a short time
Gentle people dressed so elegant
Do I truly deserve
13 years ago waiting for this day
Await the lift of heavy cloth

What have I searched for all these years?
My white curtain begins to rise I can see
Maybe the final beginning
Just the end to something new
No more way to be
For a long time
Saddened people dressed so elegant
Do I truly deserve
13 years ago waiting for this moment
Await the fall of my heavy cloth

3 year old 19 year old

When she left me
I left myself
She told me she found new love
My black curtain began to fall from my eyes
No one saw me disappear
No one saw the new me take over
Only depression set in as I wandered
    to the other side
Where faces are always hard
And no emotions are shared
Furious eyes stare at those around
While dirty looks stare back
Stranger to my family
Enemy to my friends
Lost somewhere
Never to be found, too far gone
A 19 year old stopped living life
A new 3 year old had been born unto him
This new child knew no love, no real emotion
Friends reached out their hands to him
He stared back only to look away
Family reached out to him
He looked at them and asked "who are you?"
Complete loss and anger fed this child
with wooden spoons of shame
When he did decide to leave his prison
And wander out of his shell into a new world
He was welcomed by friends and again
    they reached out to him

Their empty hands left dangling empty
    through out the dark nights
No one could reach him, too far gone
People whispered
People left him
People stopped calling
Cities he saw, turned to memories
As the future awoke the sun each morning
This young child had learned to destroy the truth
He lived on the edge of deception
But there is no way of deceiving or lying forever
One day, when he was walking
    in Edinburgh, Scotland
His black hair hiding his eyes
He turned a corner and bumped into
    another long haired man
Completely identical to himself
Only he was lost and the other was searching
A look of sadness dropped from his face
They both removed the hair from his eyes
A smile took shape on his lips
And a hand was extended
The 3 year old reached out and shook it
They hugged each other
The 19 year old whispered "welcome back,
    I have searched all over for you"
The 3 year old 19 year old transformed
    into a 22 year old
Now I am truly alive again
The black curtain has disappeared

Forgotten hope

What is left inside when happiness is forgotten?
Search for answers I cannot see
And questions I do not ask
Only to see nothing while everyone sees all

When nothing is left inside and
    regrets are all you know
To give up and go on as if nothing
While everyone else goes on with all
To see blindly so as not to see at all

Reminded of never

It is called never
no reason why
I have never felt this way
And never want this to end
So the perfect name would be such
I never want to hurt you
And I never want to stop loving you

It is called always
All reasons why
I always felt alone
And always thought it would end that way
So the perfect name would be such
I always want to love you
And never be reminded of always
And always be reminded of never

Where is Heaven?

To have seen the world through my eyes
And to feel the pain as I alone have
No words can describe my thoughts
Because words were never meant to stand alone

To have understood so many as I alone have
And to love those who only hate like I once did
No feelings can be felt
Because our comfort was never real

Never said goodbye

She left me there alone
With only a kiss to remember
Said she had to go
I never said goodbye

Did she leave this place? Or is it all a dream?
With a smile, she disappeared like rain
I said nothing, nothing for her to hear

Wonder now, what I would have said
And wish I had that moment again
Only to say goodbye to my friend
Because I know I will never see her again

Do you know what killed my son?

Did this place kill him?
The saddest words I ever heard
Echoed through these walls and my head
His voice so low
The saddest eyes I ever saw

Do you know why he left here?
I only stared, no words could be shared
His lonely words made me sad
Did this place kill him?
Did these walls hear him fall?

With a flame he could end it all
He could destroy the memory of his son
His lonely voice could echo through
    these walls and my head no more
Did this place kill my son?